THE MINISTRY OF THE PROPHETIC

ISAAC WILLIAMS

Copyright 2016 © Isaac Williams

All rights reserved. No part of this publication may be produced, distributed, or transmitted in any form or by any means, including photocopying, recording, or other electronic or mechanical methods, without the prior written permision of the publisher, except in the case of brief quotations embodied in critical reviews and certain other noncommercial uses permitted by copyright law.

For permission requests, write to the publisher, addressed "Attention: Permissions Coordinator" at the email address below:

Life and Success Media Ltd
e-mail: info@abookinsideyou.com
www.abookinsideyou.com

ISBN Number: 978-1-64370-586-6
Cover Design: MIADesign.com

Prophecy: 'a message inspired by God, a divine revelation'

'Prophecy' or 'Prophesy' means to speak forth or declare the divine will, to interpret the purposes of God or to make known in any way the truth of God which is designed to influence people.

Prophecy is the testimony of Jesus and is the revelation of what is on His heart for His people. **'For the testimony of Jesus is the spirit of prophecy'** (Revelations 19:10)

Contents

1. **Introduction** 1
   a. The restoration of the prophetic 1
   b. My journey 1

2. **The prophetic gift** 7

3. **The prophetic ministry** 9
   a. Your gift will make room for you 9
   b. No training no reigning 10
   c. A prophetic heart 10
   d. Fear and faith 11

4. **Prophetic training** 13
   a. What is prophecy? 13

5. **Administration of prophecy** 15
   a. Revelation 15
   b. Interpretation 21
   c. Application 22

6. **Functioning in the gift of prophecy** 25

7. **Practical guidelines for prophetic ministry** 28

8. **The gift of prophecy the ministry of the prophet** 34

9. **The purpose of the gift of prophecy** 35

10. **The office of the prophet** 36

11. **Old and new testament prophets** 38

12. **What is the role of a prophet** 40

13. **Why God sent prophets** 42

14. **Understanding different types of prophets** 43

15. **Special features of a prophet** 45

16. **Test of a true prophet** 48

1
INTRODUCTION

The restoration of the prophetic

For over 19 years I have been ministering in the prophetic. However, in 2016 the Lord impressed on my heart the need to start training and empowering believers about the gifts of the Spirit and the ministry of a prophet. In February 2017 the Lord revealed to me in a dream that I should put together the teachings from the school of the prophets into a book so that Christians everywhere can access the bible teachings; as individuals, in groups, or in their church assemblies.

My journey

I was born in the UK in the late 1960's to Jamaican parents and going to church was a part of my early life. It was also common to many of my peers who were also born into the African Caribbean community.

I have no recollection of really liking church as a young boy apart from the odd Christmas present that I received which wasn't really that great; a pencil, a rubber or something of no importance to me anyway.

When I was about seven or eight I had an encounter with Jesus in the night at an hour I can't recall. I saw Jesus sitting down on a throne with a gold 'stick like thing' in his hand. At that time, I didn't know what a sceptre was!

When I eventually woke up I remember telling my mum "I saw Jesus last night". Her response was simply, "okay dear." Then she continued to do whatever she was doing.

At about the age of fourteen my dad gave me the choice whether to continue to go to church or not. Obviously, I jumped at the chance of never ever returning there again unless it was for a wedding or for a funeral. From that moment on my attitude was, 'world here I come!' I never looked back and I plunged into everything the world had to offer from, music, drugs and as they say, 'rock 'n' roll!'

So, how did I get to where I am today?

In short, one Saturday night, 25 years ago, just as I was entering a nightclub, I had hardly gotten through the doors when I heard a heavenly voice call to me saying, *"Isaac, what are you doing in here?"* I paused for a moment alarmed by the heavenly sound and once again I heard it, *"Isaac, what are you doing in here?"*

Strangely, I knew it was Jesus speaking to me. Why? Because, when Jesus speaks to you by the Holy Spirit, you will recognise His voice over and above any other you might have heard before or after. The bible says that ...***His voice is as the sound of many waters*** (Revelation 1:15).

The many waters represent commanding authority. After this, Jesus, through the Holy Spirit went on to say, *"Son, let me show you what's [really] going on in here."*

Suddenly a large, transparent hand positioned itself over my face and then moved across it. As the hand moved, the Holy Spirit unveiled dark spirit figures before my eyes that were the inspiration behind everyone that was dancing in the club.

The bible says… *'and the whole world lies under the sway of the wicked one'*(1 John 5:19).

From that moment I just stood against a wall in the club. I don't remember much else as the shock of that revelation took its toll. Eventually I made my way back home in the early hours of the morning and fell asleep.

The next morning I received a call from my younger brother and he shared something with me that to the reader might seem trivial. He said that he had met two young Christian guys who dressed in a style similar to how we dressed. Now any reader must be wondering, *"what's significant about meeting two young Christian guys who dressed like me and my brother did?"* I will explain.

You see at that time, I was extremely fashion conscious and my personal view of any young person around my own age who was confessing to be a Christian was that they had no fun in life and they all seemed to dress as if they had little or no fashion sense, wearing tweed jackets and flared trousers! There was nothing about them that made me want what they said they had. So, to hear my brother say that he had met two young Christian guys who 'dressed like we did', was shocking to me as I never imagined that you could be a Christian and dress fashionably too!

The following day in September 1992, I had given my life to the Lord Jesus Christ.

Late one night about six months later, I woke up suddenly with an overwhelming feeling on the inside of me that led me to cry out, *"Who am I?"* I don't know where this came from and went back to sleep.

In the book Ecclesiastics 3:11 (The Amplified Bible) it says that **He (God) has planted eternity in men's hearts and minds (a divinely implanted sense of a PURPOSE working through the ages which nothing under the sun but God alone can satisfy).**

Not too long after this I heard the Holy spirit say to me, *"Isaac, you are my* **Prophet***"*. I remember waking up shortly afterwards and thinking, *"what is God talking about, and what is a* **Prophet?***"*

Just like Moses I found myself trying to find out the meaning of my true existence. However, as time went on I started to develop my understanding of the prophetic ministry under the guidance of my church.

A few years later I again had a strange encounter with the Lord.

One morning I was on my way to work when the Spirit of the Lord started compelling me to look at the buildings that were around me, and then the Holy Spirit said;

"Isaac, one day I am going to give you a building and it will be an Evangelical School, it is for the teaching and the preaching of Jesus Christ, and you are to teach and train God's people."

I found it hard to believe and I replied by saying that this was not going to happen because there was no way God could use someone like me to teach and train people! How wrong was I. By 1998, I had become an ordained Pastor.

Not long after that, the Spirit of the Lord reminded me of the earlier prophecy concerning teaching and training people and added that the vision for the church was;

"to equip the saints for the work of the Lord" **(Ephesians 4 v 12)**

The Holy Spirit went on to say that Pastoring would be the means by which I would fulfil the call on my life and see the unfolding of all that God had said to me in the past.

I've now been in ministry for twenty years at the time of writing and I've watched the almighty God by his Holy Spirit use this insecure boy and take His time with me to develop my character and the prophetic ministry that He has called me to.

'And He Himself gave some to be apostles, some prophets, some evangelists, some pastors and teachers.' *(***Ephesians 4:11)**

2

THE PROPHETIC GIFT

When Jesus Christ ascended upon high He gave five major gifts to the Church, and one of those was the ministry of the prophet. The authority and calling of the prophetic ministry has become more widely acceptable in the 21st century church. However there are different dimensions of the prophetic ministry so everyone in Christendom has the opportunity to participate.

..to another the working of miracles, to another prophecy, to another discerning of spirits, to another different kinds of tongues, to another the interpretation of tongues (1 Corinthians 12:10)

3

THE PROPHETIC MINISTRY

If you are called to any type of prophetic ministry the first thing you need to know is that your calling does not make you superior to anyone else. Some members of the body of Christ may presume if you do have a prophetic gift/calling that you have the answer to everybody's issues. This is far from the truth and must not be encouraged.

Your gift will make room for you

'Man's gift makes room for him, and brings him before great men' (Proverbs 18:16).

If you have a gift, it will make room for itself. Leaders and ministers will begin to recognise your gift. God will open doors to you. He is the One who called you and He can bring His call to fruition in your life. Be careful not to fall into the trap of some and attempt to launch your own ministry outside of the biblical pattern set out in scripture.

And if ye have not been faithful in that which is another man's, who shall give you that which is your own? (Luke 16:12)

No training no reigning

1 And the sons of the prophets said to Elisha, "See now, the place where we dwell with you is too small for us. 2 Please, let us go to the Jordan, and let every man take a beam from there, and let us make there a place where we may dwell." (2 Kings 6:1-2)

Development is important in any type of work or ministry. When it comes to the prophetic you need to be connected to those that will give you room to grow, make mistakes and impart to you and validate your calling…'*As they ministered to the Lord and fasted, the Holy Spirit said, "Now separate to Me Barnabas and Saul for the work to which I have called them."* (Act 13:2)

A prophetic heart (The heart of God concerning a matter)

Prophetic people ought to live according to what is written in 1 Corinthians 13:2…'*Though I have the gift of prophecy, and understand all mysteries and all knowledge, and though I have all faith, so that I could remove mountains, but have not love, I am nothing.*'

Your gift is not as important as the people to whom you minister. When we lose sight of what Godly ministry is all about we forget that we are all called to be ambassadors of the Lord…***Now then, we are ambassadors for Christ* (2 Corinthians 5:20)**

Fear and faith

...Gideon threshed wheat in the winepress, in order to hide it from the Midianites. ^12 And the Angel of the Lord appeared to him, and said to him, "The Lord is with you, you mighty man of valour!" (Judges 6:11-12)

Gideon was hiding in a winepress because he was fearful. However the winepress was not the place that God had in mind for Gideon's full potential to be realised, so Gideon needed to be coached out of fear by words of encouragement to help him make the exchange from fear and doubt to faith in God because...' **perfect love casts out fear'** (1 John 4:18).

So God called Gideon a champion, right where he stood, even in his own human limitations. This was the first step toward changing Gideon's perspective of himself and moving him into his God ordained purpose. ...**For I know the thoughts that I think toward you, says the Lord, thoughts of peace and not of evil, to give you a future and a hope** (Jeremiah 29:11).

Fear will always try to hinder your move into the prophetic. Questions like; "Am I really hearing God?" "What if I get it wrong?" and "What will people think of me?"

Gods plan is that we learn and develop within the boundaries and the safety of His church. Each church/assembly should have ministry teams that can provide relevant guidance and training for gifts and callings. In the Old Testament they had '*a school of prophets'*; 1 Samuel 19:18-24 2 Kings 2 and 2 Kings 4:38-44 (Some biblical translations say 'company of prophets' or 'sons of the prophets').

1 Samuel chapter 19 tells the story of King Saul who sends messengers to arrest David. When these men meet '*a company of prophets*' under Samuel's leadership, the King's men also prophesied. This occurred three times. Eventually King Saul went to David himself and ended up prophesying too, leading people to ask, "**Is Saul also among the prophets?**" 1 Samuel 19:24. This became a saying in those days.

The '*company of prophets*' in 1 Samuel 19, were students of the prophet Samuel.

In 2 Kings Chapter 2 when Elijah was traveling with Elisha, a group of prophets from Bethel told Elisha that Elijah, his teacher would be taken from him that day (verse 3). When Elisha and Elijah came to Jericho another group of prophets also repeated the same prophecy (verse 5), and finally a third group of prophets. Jordan River also conveyed the same message (verse 7). So, we find different groups of prophets all from separate locations Bethel, Jericho and near the Jordan River; all these different groups of prophets relied on the guidance and leadership of the chief Prophet Elijah.

In 2 Kings 4:38-41, Elisha the prophet is in Gilgal throughout a time of extreme famine. Under the influence of the Holy Spirit Elisha miraculously changes an inedible stew into an edible dish for this group of prophets indicating his role as care giver for the prophets in Gilgal.

So, it is clear that there were **schools of the prophets** whose pupils were known as sons of the prophets and as trainees who followed the teachings of Samuel, Elijah, and Elisha during the time of the prophets.

4

PROPHETIC TRAINING

I t shall come to pass in the last days, says God, that I will pour out of My Spirit on all flesh; Your sons and your daughters shall prophesy, your young men shall see visions, your old men shall dream dreams...18 I will pour out My Spirit in those days; and they shall prophesy...20 before the coming of the great and awesome day of the LORD. (Acts 2:17-20).

All are called to prophecy and to function in the gifts of the Spirit; all nations and men and women alike.

What is prophecy?

The spiritual gift of prophecy is listed among the gifts of the Spirit in

1 Corinthians 12:10. The Greek word translated 'prophesy' or 'prophecy' in both passages correctly means to 'speak forth or declare the divine will, to interpret the purposes of God, or to make known in any way the truth of God which is designed to influence people.'

Prophecy is the testimony of Jesus and is the revelation of what is on His heart for His people. *'For the testimony of Jesus is the spirit of prophecy'* (Revelations 19:10).

The first rule of prophetic ministry is that it does not contradict the written word of God. Believers can find themselves in danger when they put the supernatural above Gods written word. This happens when an element of supernatural truth is spoken but no time is given to study the Holy Scriptures for ourselves that relate to the 'supernatural truths' that we hear. We can then be open to any so called prophetic word or move of God without testing if we have actually heard from God.

'Heaven and earth will pass away, but My words will by no means pass away' (Matthew 24:35)

[16]*All Scripture is given by inspiration of God, and is profitable for doctrine, for reproof, for correction, for instruction in righteousness,* [17] *that the man of God may be complete, thoroughly equipped for every good work* (2 Timothy 3:16-17)

Test all things; hold fast what is good (1 Thessalonians 5:21)

5

ADMINISTRATION OF PROPHECY

Administration of prophecy includes: revelation, interpretation, and application. Let's look at each one in turn to understand them better.

REVELATION:

Refers to receiving prophetic information (the scriptures, impressions, dreams and visions) *For we know in part and we prophesy in part* (1 Cor. 13:9).

> Hearing Gods voice is the privilege of every believer; *My sheep hear My voice, and I know them, and they follow Me (John 10:27). I have called you friends, for all things that I heard from My Father I have made known to you* (John 15:15).

The main way that we hear the voice of the Lord is through the bible or scripture. It is also the measuring stick by which we judge everything especially prophetic words that we believe have come from the Lord. ***All Scripture is given by inspiration of God, and is profitable for doctrine, for reproof, for correction, for instruction in righteousness, that the man of God may be complete, thoroughly equipped for every good work*** (2 Tim.16-17)

God speaks to us through our life circumstances and our experiences.

^{5} Now therefore, thus says the Lord of hosts: "Consider your ways ^{6} You have sown much, and bring in little; You eat, but do not have enough; You drink, but you are not filled with drink; You clothe yourselves, but no one is warm; And he who earns wages, Earns wages to put into a bag with holes." (Haggai 1:5-6)

Dreams and visions were common ways for God to speak throughout the Old Testament in the bible, e.g. Jacob, Joseph, Daniel, Jeremiah and more. Dreams and visions are also the birthright of all believers under the New Covenant so we should expect God to speak to His church today in the same way.

'And it shall come to pass in the last days, says God, That I will pour out of My Spirit on all flesh; Your sons and your daughters shall prophesy, Your young men shall see visions, Your old men shall dream dreams (Acts 2:17).

One definition of a dream according to the English Oxford dictionary, is 'a series of thoughts, images, and sensations occurring in a person's mind during sleep'

The **conscious mind** is the part of your mind that is responsible for logic and reasoning. If I asked you what one plus one equals, your conscious mind would be used to easily calculate the answer.

The conscious mind also controls all the actions that you do intentionally. For example, when you decide to make any voluntary action like getting up off your sofa to exercise, this movement is done by your conscious mind. So whenever you are aware of the thing you're doing you can be confident that you are doing it through your conscious mind.

In contrast, the **subconscious mind** is the part of your mind responsible for all of your involuntary or uncontrolled actions such as your breathing, your heart beat and your DREAMS. These are all controlled by your subconscious mind.

Your emotions are also controlled by your subconscious mind. That's why you might sometimes feel afraid, anxious or down **without wanting to experience such a feeling**.

The best way to understand the subconscious mind is to look at the example of the person who wants to learn how to drive a car. During the early stages of learning the learner might not be able to hold a conversation with anyone while driving as they need to focus fully on the task at hand – driving! However after years of driving you will find that you are able to drive around without having to overly concentrate on what you are doing.

So, there are 3 types of dreams:
1. Godly inspired
2. Demonic
3. Your dreams

Godly inspired dreams

A Godly dream or vision should fit certain characteristics; they should contain nothing that is opposed to biblical teaching and the results of the dreams should glorify God.

God uses dreams in the bible to reveal His plans, to provide information that was unavailable or that we could not know unless God had revealed it, and as a form of encouragement.

Demonic dreams

Demonic dreams can suggest thoughts and ideas that oppose biblical teaching and the results of the dreams (visions) are designed to frighten or deceive you into thinking your dream or vision is right or from God!.

In Job 4:12-16 (NIV) – A demonic dream influences Jobs friends to think wrongly about him! *'A word was secretly brought to me, my ears caught a whisper of it [13] Amid disquieting dreams in the night, when deep sleep falls on people, [14] fear and trembling seized me and made all my bones shake. [15] A spirit glided past my face, and the hair on my body stood on end. [16] It stopped, but I could not tell what it was. A form stood before my eyes, and I heard a hushed voice...*

In Job 7:13-15 - A demonic dream causes Job to think it is God who's frightening him with nightmares.

When I think my bed will comfort me and my couch will ease my complaint, 14 even then you frighten me with dreams and terrify me with visions, 15 so that I prefer strangling and death, rather than this body of mine.

Your Dreams (based on your day, situations or those that are complete nonsense)

These kinds of dreams fit the characteristics of your day to day life, past or current situations. They are not necessarily anything to do with God or the demonic but can simply be a complete nonsense - a cow flying above you, being able to take on ten men in a fight then flying away like your favourite super hero!

How did God use dreams and visions in the Bible?

Abraham (Genesis 15:1): God used a vision to restate the Abrahamic Covenant, reminding Abram that he would have a son and be the father of many nations.

Joseph (Genesis 37:1-11): Joseph is one of the most famous dreamers and dream-interpreters, in the Bible. His first recorded dreams are found in Genesis 37. They showed through easily deciphered symbols that Joseph's family would one day bow to him out of respect. His brothers didn't appreciate the dream and in their hatred sold Joseph into slavery. Eventually, through various situations, Joseph became the 2nd most powerful man in Egypt, Pharaohs right hand man.

In the New Testament, visions also provided information that was unavailable elsewhere. For instance, God used visions and dreams to identify Jesus to us and to establish His church.

[18] Now the birth of Jesus Christ was as follows: After His mother Mary was betrothed to Joseph, before they came together, she was found with child of the Holy Spirit. [19] Then Joseph her husband, being a just man, and not wanting to make her a public example, was minded to put her away secretly. [20] But while he thought about these things, behold, an angel of the Lord appeared to him in a dream, saying, "Joseph, son of David, do not be afraid to take to you Mary your wife, for that which is conceived in her is of the Holy Spirit. [21] And she will bring forth a Son, and you shall call His name Jesus, for He will save His people from their sins."

[22] So all this was done that it might be fulfilled which was spoken by the Lord through the prophet, saying: [23] "Behold, the virgin shall be with child, and bear a Son, and they shall call His name Immanuel," which is translated, "God with us." [24] Then Joseph, being aroused from sleep, did as the angel of the Lord commanded him and took to him his wife, [25] and did not know her till she had brought forth her firstborn Son. And he called His name Jesus. **(Matthew 1:18-25)**

The Apostle, Paul had several visions in his missionary career. One sent him to preach in Macedonia **(Act 16:9-10)**. Another encouraged him to keep preaching in Corinth **(Act 18:9-11)**. God also gave him a vision of heaven. **(2 Corinthians 12:1-6)**.

Angelic Visitations

Visiting angels were common in the days of the Old Testament and continues in the New Testament church.

²¹ yes, while I was speaking in prayer, the man Gabriel, whom I had seen in the vision at the beginning, being caused to fly swiftly, reached me about the time of the evening offering. ²² And he informed me, and talked with me, and said, "O Daniel, I have now come forth to give you skill to understand" (Daniel 9:21-22).

¹¹ Then an angel of the Lord appeared to him, standing on the right side of the altar of incense. ¹² And when Zacharias saw him, he was troubled, and fear fell upon him. ¹³ But the angel said to him, "Do not be afraid, Zacharias, for your prayer is heard; and your wife Elizabeth will bear you a son, and you shall call his name John." (Luke 1:11-17).

²⁶ Now an angel of the Lord spoke to Philip, saying, "Arise and go toward the south along the road which goes down from Jerusalem to Gaza." This is desert (Acts 8:26).

Audible Voice

Sometimes God will speak audibly from heaven. This is not a predominant way in which God communicates to us, so when he does it may be because the message is really important.

And suddenly a voice came from heaven, saying, "This is My beloved Son, in whom I am well pleased." (Matthew 3:17)

²⁷ "Now My soul is troubled, and what shall I say? 'Father, save Me from this hour?' But for this purpose I came to this hour. ²⁸ Father, glorify Your name." Then a voice came from heaven, saying, "I have both glorified it and will glorify it again." (John 12:27-33).

■ INTERPRETATION:

This concerns understanding revelatory information. However it is easy to give a wrong understanding of an interpretation. As an example dreams and vision can be very symbolic so unless you can really bear witness to an interpretation you should refrain from bringing one until the circumstances develop that bring its fulfillment.

In Ephesians 1:18, it talks about...***the eyes of your understanding being enlightened.*** Whenever the Spirit of the Lord shows us hidden information it is important that we seek Him to find out what it means so that we get the correct interpretation of the message.

Normally the Lord will reveal fragments of information because He wants to lead us to pray for an individual or a group of people. We should always ask questions about what we have heard and wait while expecting to receive answers from Him.

Call to Me, and I will answer you, and show you great and mighty things, which you do not know (Jeremiah 33:3).

■ APPLICATION:

This refers to rightly applying information that is interpreted, according to wisdom.

Get wisdom! Get understanding (Proverbs 4:5).

If any of you lacks wisdom, let him ask of God, who gives to all liberally and without reproach, and it will be given to him. (James 1:5).

Wisdom is always needed to rightly apply the information that is interpreted. So the questions we need to ask include:

Can I share this prophetic word?

This is where submission and accountability comes into play. There are too many stories in the body of Christ where someone has given a prophetic word without it first being submitted to a more mature believer for testing. After testing then the prophetic word can be given to the hearers whether to leaders, individuals, prayer/intercessory teams or the whole church.

Test all things; hold fast what is good (1 Thessalonians 5:21).

How much of the prophetic word is to be shared, some or all?

[16] Jesus said to her, "Go, call your husband, and come here." [17] The woman answered and said, "I have no husband." Jesus said to her, "You have well said, 'I have no husband,' [18] for you have had five husbands, and the one whom you now have is not your husband; in that you spoke truly (John 4:16-18).

In verse 4:16 the woman had just asked Jesus for this fountain of water which would spring up into everlasting life. Jesus told her to go and call her husband. Why? Jesus knew prophetically all about the sinful life she had lived, and He was going to lead her, gradually, to see it for herself.

In verse 4:17 the woman tried to suppress the truth without telling a lie. She said, "I have no husband." According to a legal sense, her testimony was true. But it was intended to hide the fact that she was then living in sin with a man who happened to not be her husband.

To keep Christ at bay she attempted to shut the door on a deeper discussion concerning her relationships. However, Jesus had full prophetic insight of her situation and knew how much He could share at a time, and in this situation He knew to unfold all. Therefore He said to her, "You have well said, 'I have no husband.'" So, while she might have been able to fool others, she was not able to fool Christ.

In verse 4:18 we see that the Lord never used His complete prophetic insightof the woman, to expose or shame her. Instead He used it to free her from the bondage of sin and to bless her with His living water.

6

FUNCTIONING IN THE GIFT OF PROPHECY

The Son can do nothing of Himself, but what He sees the Father do (John 5:19).

Principle: the demonstration of the Holy Spirit follows after a prophetic word is given from the mouth of a believer.

Prophetic information can come as a very subtle impression or imprint on our minds that indicate what the Lord intends to do regarding people or in a particular situation.

Emotional stirrings: is when you start to feel diverse emotions such as joy, sadness, or a burden for another person or a ministry. This feeling is a sign that the Lord will touch others related to that emotion or burden... ***Oh my soul, my soul! I am pained in my very heart! My heart makes a noise in me, that I cannot hold my peace, because you have heard, O my soul, the sound of the trumpet, the alarm of war.*** (Jeremiah 4:19)

Sympathetic pains: Through this motivational gift, God makes believers aware of the needs that He wants to meet through them, for His glory. Then, believers can minister to others in ways that go beyond mere human capability. One of the extraordinary ways that the Holy spirit can manifest this gift includes a sense of pain in a particular part of your body as a sign that the Lord desires to heal the disease or pain that others are feeling in that part of their body...***he who shows mercy, with cheerfulness*** (Romans 12:8).

Physical sensations: In this situation you may start to feel the Spirit's presence as either heat, fire, wind, or more, in a particular area of your body or through your five senses (e.g. smell or taste). This is an indicator that the Lord wants to touch others in a way that is related to the physical impression that you are experiencing...***And suddenly there came a sound from heaven, as of a rushing mighty wind, and it filled the whole house where they were sitting*** (Act 2:2)

Yet you do not have because you do not ask. (James 4:2)

We often do not have prophetic impressions simply because we do not ask for them. The simple act of asking makes us receptive and alert to what the Holy Spirit is doing and positions us to receive the Spirit's impressions.

Hearing the voice of the Holy Spirit often begins as a still small sound or as a subtle impression to our spirit. It can take some time to recognise the Spirit's subtle voice and for this reason many believers do not recognize or value it. However if we continue to grow and appreciate God's still small voice, we will become more attentive to it.

Behold, the LORD passed by, and a great and strong wind tore into the mountains and broke the rocks in pieces before the LORD, but the LORD was not in the wind; and after the wind an earthquake, but the LORD was not in the earthquake; 12 and after the earthquake a fire, but the LORD was not in the fire; and after the fire a still small voice. (1 Kings 19:11-12)

First, we function in the prophetic by being willing to express what we believe the Holy Spirit tells us. This requires faith…***But without faith it is impossible to please Him*** (Hebrews 11:6)

Second, we quiet our soul to listen or discern the impressions of the Spirit. ***Be silent in the LORD's presence and wait patiently for him*** (Psalm 37:7).

Finally, do not worry about missing it. We should be more concerned about never functioning in the gift of the prophetic than making a mistake! The more significant question is not, "what if I miss it?" but "what if I miss a chance to release God's prophetic voice to someone in need?"

PRACTICAL GUIDELINES FOR PROPHETIC MINISTRY

It is important to have an attitude of expectancy about the fulfilment of a prophecy. However, the way that God brings about a word that He speaks in our lives is often very different to how we might expect it to happen.

If there is uncertainty about what a particular revelation might mean, then you should put it "on the shelf" until you have a clear interpretation. It is always good practice to write prophecies down until they come to pass and go over them as often as possible to strengthen your faith and remind you of your future hope.

So then faith comes by hearing, and hearing by the word of God **(Romans 10:17)**

² Then the Lord answered me and said: "Write the vision And make it plain on tablets, That he may run who reads it. ³ For the vision is yet for an appointed time; But at the end it will speak, and it will not lie. Though it tarries, wait for it; Because it will surely come, It will not tarry (Habakkuk 2:2-3).

Having a safe atmosphere in which to operate is vital for believers. This allows room for believers to be trained, to grow in the prophetic and be in subjection to biblical protocols.

Let two or three prophets speak…30 If anything is revealed to another… let the first keep silent…32 The spirits of the prophets are subject to the prophets. 33 God is not the author of confusion but of peace…40 Let all things be done decently and in order. (1 Cor. 14:29-33, 40)

Prophetic Accountability

Prophetic accountability includes:

Being accountable:

This means we report to someone regarding revelation (prophetic insights) that we have received from the Holy Spirit.

1. *Then after fourteen years I went up again to Jerusalem with Barnabas, and also took Titus with me. 2 And I went up by revelation, and communicated to them that gospel which I preach among the Gentiles, but privately to those who were of reputation, lest by any means I might run, or had run, in vain. (Galatians 2:1-2)*

Being teachable:

This means that we are willing to learn and develop.

²⁶ So he began to speak boldly in the synagogue. When Aquila and Priscilla heard him, they took him aside and explained to him the way of God more accurately. (Acts 18:26)

Submission:

Taking heed to those who are responsible in providing spiritual oversight. (Note: I am referring to guidance that is not contrary to Biblical principles)

¹⁷ Obey those who rule over you, and be submissive, for they watch out for your souls, as those who must give account. Let them do so with joy and not with grief, for that would be unprofitable for you (Hebrews 13:17)

Signs that we are not accountable include:
- Functioning in our gifts and ministries in isolation
- Not being open to correction
- Believing we are only accountable directly to God

There are 2 types of prophecy
1. Conditional prophecy
2. Unconditional prophecy

Conditional prophecy

Conditional prophecy is when the prophecy fulfilment is reliant on the compliance of those to whom the promise is made.

Three examples can be found in Leviticus and 1 Chronicles:

1. God giving rain in due season

³ 'If you walk in My statutes and keep My commandments, and perform them, ⁴ then I will give you rain in its season, the land shall yield its produce, and the trees of the field shall yield their fruit. (Leviticus 26:3-4)

God's prophetic word to give rain to the land of Israel was based on the children of Israel walking in God's statues and keeping His commandments. Therefore, if the children of Israel did so and kept His commandments, then the prophetic word of God would come to pass. However if they chose not to do so, then the doors of the prophetic fulfilment would be closed off to them.

2. Terror and sorrow of heart for disobedience

¹⁴ 'But if you do not obey Me, and do not observe all these commandments, ¹⁵ and if you despise My statutes, or if your soul abhors My judgements, so that you do not perform all My commandments, but break My covenant, ¹⁶ I also will do this to you: I will even appoint terror over you, wasting disease and fever which shall consume the eyes and cause sorrow of heart. And you shall sow your seed in vain, for your enemies shall eat it. (Leviticus 26 14-16)

3. Healing of the land prophecy

If my people, which are called by my name, shall humble themselves, and pray, and seek my face, and turn from their wicked ways; then will I hear from heaven, and will forgive their sin, and will heal their land (2 Chronicles 7:14).

Unconditional prophecy

An unconditional prophecy is one in which there is no condition predicated. It is prophecy from God that will come to pass exactly as prophesied no matter what humans do.

Here are some examples:

1. Jesus first coming and His return

No matter what humans did, Jesus was to come to the world and He will also return. There is no question or debating whether this will happen or not. It will happen.

² "But you, Bethlehem Ephrathah, Though you are little among the thousands of Judah, Yet out of you shall come forth to Me The One to be Ruler in Israel, Whose goings forth are from of old, From everlasting." (Micah 5:2)

¹⁴ Therefore the Lord Himself will give you a sign: Behold, the virgin shall conceive and bear a Son, and shall call His name Immanuel. (Isaiah 7:14)

2. Book of Revelation

The book of Revelation is an unconditional prophecy book. The book's prophecy will be fulfilled to the dot and coma no matter what people do.

The Revelation of Jesus Christ, which God gave Him to show His servants—things which must shortly take place. (Revelation 1:1).

3. Elijah gives King Ahab an unconditional prophetic word regarding the coming of rain.

⁴¹ Then Elijah said to Ahab, "Go up, eat and drink; for there is the sound of abundance of rain."

…⁴⁴ Then it came to pass the seventh time, that he said, "There is a cloud, as small as a man's hand, rising out of the sea!" So he said, "Go up, say to Ahab, 'Prepare your chariot, and go down before the rain stops you.'"

⁴⁵ Now it happened in the meantime that the sky became black with clouds and wind, and there was a heavy rain. (1 Kings 18: 41, 45)

We are given the above examples to teach that all prophetic words that are given will completely come to pass no matter what. There are both conditional and unconditional prophetic words. The examples also prove that a true prophet of God isn't always defined by his prophecies always coming to pass! Instead there is a need to define whether the word given is a conditional or an unconditional prophecy.

THE GIFT OF PROPHECY AND THE MINISTRY OF THE PROPHET

The gift of prophecy

1 *...to another the working of miracles, to another prophecy, to another discerning of spirits, to another different kinds of tongues, to another the interpretation of tongues.* Corinthians 12:10

Having then gifts differing according to the grace that is given to us, whether prophecy, let us prophesy according to the proportion of faith; Romans 12:6

The gift of prophecy is to bring forth an inspired utterance.

9

THE PURPOSE OF THE GIFT OF PROPHECY

Three things ought to happen when prophecy is given:
1. **EDIFICATION** - The act of building, building up
2. **EXHORTATION** - Admonition, Encouragement
3. **COMFORT** - Calming and consoling

But the manifestation of the Spirit is given to each one for the profit of all: 1 Corinthians 12:7

But he who prophesies speaks edification and exhortation and comfort to men 1 Corinthians 14:3

10

THE OFFICE OF THE PROPHET

What is a prophet in the Bible?"

In a general sense, a prophet is a person who speaks God's truth to others. The English word ***prophet*** comes from the Greek word ***prophetes***, which can mean 'one who speaks forth' or 'advocate.' Prophets are also called 'seers,' because of their spiritual insight or their ability to 'see' the future.

Prophets had the charge of speaking God's Word to the people. They were instrumental in guiding the nation of Israel and in the New Testament the establishing of God's church. ***...having been built on the foundation of the apostles and prophets, Jesus Christ Himself being the chief cornerstone***(Ephesians 2:20).

In The Old Testament **Elijah** and **Elisha** both demonstrate the prophetic ministry at a high level of maturity. They not only operated individually in the prophetic gift themselves, they also trained others in their own prophetic schools. (1 Kings 20:25).

In the New Testament, Jesus Himself came as **prophet**, priest, king, and Messiah, accomplishing many of the messianic prophecies of the Old Testament.

In the early church we saw the continuation of the prophetic. As an example Ananias give a prophecy about the Apostle Paul's future, Acts 9:10 and Acts 21:9 mentions four daughters of Philip who could prophesy.

Prophecy is listed as a spiritual gift in 1 Corinthians 12 and 14. However we also need to tackle the fact that not everyone who 'speaks forth' a message is really a prophet of God. The Bible warns against **false prophets** who claim to speak for God but who are really deceivers within the church.

In the New Testament Jesus warns us against false prophets; we should *"watch out for false prophets. They come to you in sheep's clothing, but inwardly they are ferocious wolves"* (Matthew 7:15).

To avoid being led astray, it is imperative that we *"test the spirits to see whether they are from God"* (1 John 4:1).

A true prophet of God will give himself over to speaking God's truth in love. He or she will speak in line with God's Holy Scriptures.

11

OLD AND NEW TESTAMENT PROPHETS

The terms *Major Prophets* and *Minor Prophets* are basically a way to divide the Old Testament prophetic books.

The Major Prophets are Isaiah, Jeremiah, Lamentations, Ezekiel, and Daniel.

The Minor Prophets are Hosea, Joel, Amos, Obadiah, Jonah, Micah, Nahum, Habakkuk, Zephaniah, Haggai, Zechariah, and Malachi.

The Major Prophets are described as 'major' because their books are longer and the content has broad, even global implications. Major Prophets of today normally have a global prophetic ministry to different countries and may have access to Presidents and Prime Ministers.

The Minor Prophets are described as 'minor' because their books are shorter and the content is more narrowly focused. However that does not mean the Minor Prophets are any less inspired than the Major Prophets. It is merely a matter of God selecting to reveal more to the Major Prophets than He did to the Minor Prophets. Minor Prophets of today normally have a prophetic voice in their church assembly and to their local environment.

New Testament Prophets

John the Baptist, John the Revelator, Agabus, Anna, Barnabas, Paul the Apostle

12

WHAT IS THE ROLE OF A PROPHET

"I will raise up for them a Prophet like you from among their brethren, and will put My words in His mouth, and He shall speak to them all that I command Him. And it shall be that whoever will not hear My words, which He speaks in My name, I will require it of him." (Deuteronomy 18:18-19, NKJV).

God speaks to us through the prophets.

"I have also spoken by the prophets, and have multiplied visions; I have given symbols through the witness of the prophets." (Hosea 12:10)

God reveals His plans to the prophets.

"Surely the Lord GOD does nothing, unless He reveals His secret to His servants the prophets" (Amos 3:7).

We benefit if we listen to God's prophets.

"…'Hear me, O Judah and you inhabitants of Jerusalem: Believe in the LORD your God, and you shall be established; believe His prophets, and you shall prosper.'" (2 Chronicles 20:20).

13

WHY GOD SENT PROPHETS

To guide his people in the right way.

"Yet He sent prophets to them, to bring them back to the LORD; and they testified against them, but they would not listen." (2 Chronicles 24:19).

God uses prophets to lead His people and to guard them.

"By a prophet the LORD brought Israel out of Egypt, and by a prophet he was preserved." (Hosea 12:13).

Prophets are not always popular.

Blessed are you when they revile and persecute you, and say all kinds of evil against you falsely for My sake. Rejoice and be exceedingly glad, for great is your reward in heaven, for so they persecuted the prophets who were before you." (Matthew 5:11-12).

14

UNDERSTANDING DIFFERENT TYPES OF PROPHET

Prophets reflect some or all of the following characteristics and abilities:

- Can bring restoration and life, just look at what God said to Abimelech in a dream after he took Abraham's wife. **Genesis 20:7**
- are spoken of symbolically as 'an almond tree' **Jeremiah 1:11-12**, arrows and more
- flow in the spirit, word of knowledge, etc. The other gifts will be working in your life if you are prophetic
- have a strong sense of both prayer and worship, such as songs via King David
- have a unique way of interpreting scripture
- can struggle with highs and lows; **1 Kings 19:4** Elijah prayed that he might die when he was feeling down. Prophets can have traumatic

mood swings especially when the spirit lifts! Why? Because, there is a distinction between you and the Spirit of the prophetic. This means you can have moments of feeling down or weak and need character to help keep you together as well as good people around to encourage you.

15

SPECIAL FEATURES OF A PROPHET

There are also special features that prophets might possess. Here are some:

A face to face Prophet

Then He said, "Hear now My words: If there is a prophet among you, I, the Lord, make Myself known to him in a vision; I speak to him in a dream.

Not so with My servant Moses; He is faithful in all My house.

I speak with him face to face (Numbers 12:6-8)

Moses relationship with the Lord was unique. It's described as face to face, as a man speaks to his friend, whom he converses with freely and familiarly, and without any concerns. Some prophet's relationships with the Lord are closer than others.

Governmental prophets
Governmental prophets deal with government such as Elijah, Daniel, Jonah and more.

Prophets gifted in a specific area
The Bible reveals that people were moved to prophesy with and under the blessing of musical instruments:

The company of prophets had musical instruments with them when they prophesied (1 Samuel 10:5-6).

A harp was played by David to drive the evil spirit away from King Saul (1 Samuel 16:14-23, 1 Samuel 18:10)

Prophets that are master trainers
These are good at training others or pulling potential out of others.

Intercessory prophets
Abraham's Prayer for Sodom (Genesis 18:20-33)
Ezra's Prayer, Identifying With The Sins Of His People (Ezra 9:6-15)
Daniel's Prayer, Identifying With The Sins Of His People.
(Daniel 9:4-19)

Confrontational prophets
Often misunderstood, confrontational prophets do exactly that, confront. This often leads to them being misunderstood and potentially unpopular.

Warring prophets
These are good at fighting, spiritually. Elijah is a good example.

Writing & recording prophets
Prophets like this will write books and record information as God leads them to do so.

The Company of prophets
These prophets gather together and work together.

The sons of the prophets
These represent the next generation and need training and character development.

16

TEST OF A TRUE PROPHET

¹ If there arises among you a prophet or a dreamer of dreams, and he gives you a sign or a wonder, ² and the sign or the wonder comes to pass, of which he spoke to you, saying, 'Let us go after other gods'—which you have not known—'and let us serve them,' ³ you shall not listen to the words of that prophet or that dreamer of dreams, for the Lord your God is testing you to know whether you love the Lord your God with all your heart and with all your soul. (Deuteronomy 13:1-3)

¹ Beloved, do not believe every spirit, but test the spirits, whether they are of God; because many false prophets have gone out into the world. ² By this you know the Spirit of God: Every spirit that confesses that Jesus Christ has come in the flesh is of God, ³ and every spirit that does not confess that Jesus Christ has come in the flesh is not of God. And this is the spirit of the Antichrist, which you have heard was coming, and is now already in the world (1 John 4:1-3).

Do what God tells you to do regardless of people (1 Kings 13:1-24)

1   *And behold, a man of God (An unnamed Prophet) went from Judah to Bethel by the word of the Lord, and Jeroboam stood by the altar to burn incense.*

2   *Then he cried out against the altar by the word of the Lord, and said, "O altar, altar! Thus says the Lord: 'Behold, a child, Josiah by name, shall be born to the house of David; and on you he shall sacrifice the priests of the high places who burn incense on you, and men's bones shall be burned on you."*

3   *And he gave a sign the same day, saying, "This is the sign which the Lord has spoken: Surely the altar shall split apart, and the ashes on it shall be poured out."*

4   *So it came to pass when King Jeroboam heard the saying of the man of God, who cried out against the altar in Bethel, that he stretched out his hand from the altar, saying, "Arrest him!" Then his hand, which he stretched out toward him, withered, so that he could not pull it back to himself.*

5   *The altar also was split apart, and the ashes poured out from the altar, according to the sign which the man of God had given by the word of the Lord.*

6   *Then the king answered and said to the man of God, "Please entreat the favor of the Lord your God, and pray for me, that my hand may be restored to me." So the man of God entreated the Lord, and the king's hand was restored to him, and became as before.*

7   *Then the king said to the man of God, "Come home with me and refresh yourself, and I will give you a reward."*

8   But the man of God said to the king, "If you were to give me half your house, I would not go in with you; nor would I eat bread nor drink water in this place.

9   For so it was commanded me by the word of the Lord, saying, 'You shall not eat bread, nor drink water, nor return by the same way you came.'"

10   So he went another way and did not return by the way he came to Bethel.

11   Now an old prophet dwelt in Bethel, and his sons came and told him all the works that the man of God had done that day in Bethel; they also told their father the words which he had spoken to the king.

12   And their father said to them, "Which way did he go?" For his sons had seen which way the man of God went who came from Judah.

13   Then he said to his sons, "Saddle the donkey for me." So they saddled the donkey for him; and he rode on it,

14   and went after the man of God, and found him sitting under an oak. Then he said to him, "Are you the man of God who came from Judah?" And he said, "I am."

15   Then he said to him, "Come home with me and eat bread."

16   And he said, "I cannot return with you nor go in with you; neither can I eat bread nor drink water with you in this place.

17   For I have been told by the word of the Lord, 'You shall not eat bread nor drink water there, nor return by going the way you came.'"

18 He said to him, "I too am a prophet as you are, and an angel spoke to me by the word of the Lord, saying, 'Bring him back with you to your house, that he may eat bread and drink water.' " (He was lying to him.)

19 So he went back with him, and ate bread in his house, and drank water.

20 Now it happened, as they sat at the table, that the word of the Lord came to the prophet who had brought him back;

21 and he cried out to the man of God who came from Judah, saying, "Thus says the Lord: 'Because you have disobeyed the word of the Lord, and have not kept the commandment which the Lord your God commanded you,

22 but you came back, ate bread, and drank water in the place of which the Lord said to you, Eat no bread and drink no water, your corpse shall not come to the tomb of your fathers.

23 So it was, after he had eaten bread and after he had drunk, that he saddled the donkey for him, the prophet whom he had brought back.

24 When he was gone, a lion met him on the road and killed him. And his corpse was thrown on the road, and the donkey stood by it. The lion also stood by the corpse.

1 Kings 13 talks about a young prophet who is meant to rebuke the king then make his way home a certain way however he listened to an older prophet and ended up dead with a lion standing over him.

You need to know how God uses you no matter what others might say. **Stay true to YOUR calling!**

www.ingramcontent.com/pod-product-compliance
Lightning Source LLC
Chambersburg PA
CBHW052120070526
44584CB00017B/2572